Machines with Power!
Fire Trucks

by Amy McDonald

BLASTOFF! Beginners

BELLWETHER MEDIA
MINNEAPOLIS, MN

Blastoff! Beginners are developed by literacy experts and educators to meet the needs of early readers. These engaging informational texts support young children as they begin reading about their world. Through simple language and high frequency words paired with crisp, colorful photos, Blastoff! Beginners launch young readers into the universe of independent reading.

Blastoff! Universe

Reading Level — Grade K

Grades 1-3

Grade 4

Sight Words in This Book 🔍

a	go	make	them	way
are	have	must	they	who
can	help	on	this	
come	here	out	to	
for	in	people	up	
get	is	the	water	

This edition first published in 2021 by Bellwether Media, Inc.

No part of this publication may be reproduced in whole or in part without written permission of the publisher. For information regarding permission, write to Bellwether Media, Inc., Attention: Permissions Department, 6012 Blue Circle Drive, Minnetonka, MN 55343.

Library of Congress Cataloging-in-Publication Data

LC record for Fire Trucks available at https://lccn.loc.gov/2020007390

Text copyright © 2021 by Bellwether Media, Inc. BLASTOFF! BEGINNERS and associated logos are trademarks and/or registered trademarks of Bellwether Media, Inc.

Editor: Christina Leaf   Designer: Andrea Schneider

Printed in the United States of America, North Mankato, MN.

Table of Contents

What Are Fire Trucks?

Fire! Fire!
Who can help?
Here comes
a fire truck!

Fire trucks are
fast machines.
They help
put out fires.

Parts of a Fire Truck

Fire trucks have ladders. Ladders take people up.

ladder

FIRE RESCUE

Fire trucks have **hoses**. Hoses get water to the fire.

hose

Fire trucks have lights. Lights mean the truck is coming.

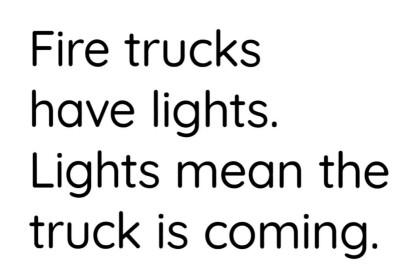

lights

Fire trucks have **sirens**. Sirens mean make way!

siren

Fire Trucks at Work

Fire trucks must go fast! Firefighters ride in them.

Fire trucks hold **gear**. They have tools for firefighters.

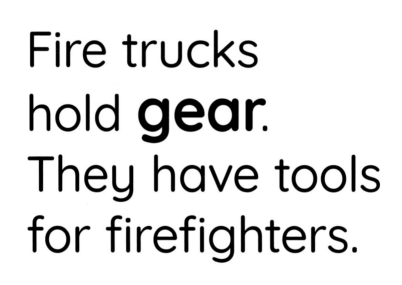

gear

This truck is
off to a fire.
Hold on!

Fire Truck Facts

Fire Truck Parts

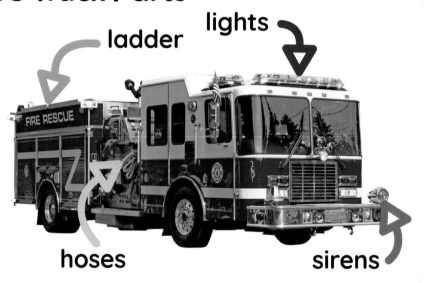

ladder

lights

hoses

sirens

Fire Truck Jobs

put out fires

carry firefighters

bring gear

Glossary

gear

the tools
firefighters use

hoses

tubes that
carry water

sirens

machines that
make loud sounds
to warn others

To Learn More

ON THE WEB

FACTSURFER

Factsurfer.com gives you a safe, fun way to find more information.

1. Go to www.factsurfer.com.

2. Enter "fire trucks" into the search box and click 🔍.

3. Select your book cover to see a list of related content.

Index

The images in this book are reproduced through the courtesy of: ryasick, front cover; Roberto Galan, p. 3; poco_bw, pp. 4-5; Avatar_023, pp. 6-7; vectorarts, p. 8 (ladder); GaryTalton, pp. 8-9, 14-15; Grigorev_Vladmir, p. 10 (hose); egd, pp. 10-11; Jose Luis Carrascosa, pp. 12-13; oneinchpunch, pp. 16-17; Carl Miller/ Alamy Stock Photo, pp. 18-19; Joe_Potato, pp. 20-21; Le Do, p. 22 (parts); Sjo, p. 22 (put out fires); LPettet, p. 22 (carry firefighters); Jill Morgan/ Alamy Stock Photo, p. 22 (bring gear); VanderWolf-Images, p. 23 (gear); Fotografiche, p. 23 (hoses); Images-USA/ Alamy Stock Photo, p. 23 (sirens).